Out of the Closet

Into the Light

2nd Edition
Jewel of the West Publishing

ISBN-13: 978-0615807645
ISBN-10: 061580764X
Library of Congress Control Number: 2013938677

Cover Design by
Middtown Productions
www.middtownproductions.com

Out of the Closet

Into the Light

J. Adams

As told by

Jordan Jantz

From Jordan:

To my guardian angels,

Christian Thad Adams

and

Henry Stuart Matis,

who walk with me in spirit.

From Me:

To all those who feel trapped

and imprisoned in the past,

and still bear the scars.

May you break free,

allow healing to begin,

and discover your wings!

A Word

We all have trials in this life, some more than others. We can either grow from them and allow them to shape us into great men and women, or we can let those trials set our course in life, taking us to the darkest of places.

This book is about an amazingly-tragic life that started in that darkest of places, yet traveled through a long, cold, seemingly-endless night into the light of the sun. This story is not for the faint of heart, because it is of an existence created in the worst nightmares, and it is raw, disturbing, and unapologetic.

But it is the truth.

This is Jordan's story.

But whoso shall offend one of these little ones which believe in me, it were better for him that a millstone were hanged about his neck, and that he were drowned in the depth of the sea.

Matthew 18: 6

Though the names have been changed to protect the innocent, and the guilty, the story is true and the events actually happened.

February 25, 2013

When I look back on my life, it is a miracle that I made it through all that happened. It seems like a nightmare I've barely woken from. The faces and places are still fresh in my mind, the shades and colors as vivid as ever. The sights and smells come back at times, drawing my thoughts to days long gone, times never to be revisited.

I have talked about my life before, but not in this much depth, and not with my family. Friends are appalled by the events I have shared, and other friends I have known for years wonder why I've never opened up before this. My answer is always, "I never wanted pity because there are so many others who have probably experienced worse things."

There have been many closet doors in my life that have hidden many things, and I managed to walk through them all, struggling to leave the painful experiences that lay behind them, experiences shrouded in darkness, hidden from the eyes of those who would clearly see them for what they were, and clearly see me for what I was.

To this day, there are moments when the flashbacks that occur are so strong, I literally lose control of my bodily functions. If I am standing in the grocery store and see a small child angrily chastised or hear a family yelling, or watch the news and a child has been kidnapped, raped, or murdered, it takes me back to those dark days. The shame and embarrassment I feel at these times is overwhelming. I see a therapist regularly. I take prescribed anxiety medication during the day and sleeping medication at night just to function. It is the only way I can live some semblance of a normal life.

However, one thing above all helps me through each new day. And that is my knowledge that no matter how rough it gets or how abandoned I still feel at times, God is there. The Savior is with me. As long as I hold to the light, I will never be alone again.

So now everything is out in the open, never again to be shut away, covered or hidden. There are no more secrets, no animosity or anger; there is only the sweet peace of healing and knowing that the old life of my memories is no longer mine, that those burdens are no longer mine. Someone else carries them now.

And I can go on.

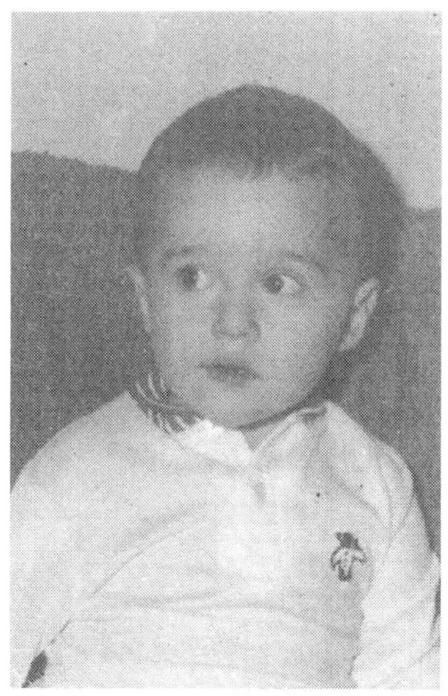

One

World of Darkness

Decatur, Illinois

When we come into this world, we hope to have parents who will love, lead, guide, and teach us what we should know. We are completely dependent upon them for care and compassion, comfort, stability, and nurturing. All of these things are necessary to give a child a sense of home. All are necessary to give a sense of family.

I had none of these things.

When I was born, I was given the name James

Lee Bond. The year was 1959. Looking back, I have to wonder why my biological parents had me. It didn't seem like they liked me or even wanted me. At least Mama didn't. Nothing made that more clear than when she gave me away years later.

I had two brothers and a sister. I was the middle child. Mama and Daddy were not always together and it seemed theirs was a 'sometimes' relationship. I can't really call them parents because that would involve caring for me as their child. Their parenting skills were as far from the *best* as they could possibly be. My mother was abusive and the perpetrator of the worst kind of neglect.

I was a very hyper-active child and would have been labeled ADD if the term had existed back then, and the way she decided to handle my 'condition' was to keep me locked in a broom closet.

For two years I lived in this closet, and the sounds of the door rattling, locking and unlocking, burn in my memory. The darkness actually made my hearing acute and that rattling always frightened me because I never knew what to expect, which made me lose it emotionally sometimes. I had no real interaction with anyone in the family and I didn't know how to talk because I was never taught. Nor was I toilet trained, therefore I lived in my own feces and was left to my own devices. Does a two-year-old even have devices of any kind? Not that I know of, but I digress. I still remember that pungent smell well. It soaked into my skin, the odor filling my nose constantly. The only light in my confined world was the small sliver of brightness under the door. Other than that, I lived in total darkness. I was completely lost.

My food was slid under the door on a plate and I could never see what I was eating. I only knew that I was hungry, so I would crawl through my own waste to get to the food. Because thirst was always a problem, I would feel for wetness on the floor and drink it, not knowing if it was water or urine. But I guess it didn't really matter. Everything was the same in the dark.

The only time the door was opened was when my mother came in and gave me my weekly hosing off while giving the floor a good bleaching. The water was always frigid and the abrupt light so blinding, I would cry out, completely stunned and disoriented. Whenever I screamed for help, she immediately covered my mouth, told me I was ugly, and plunged me back into darkness.

It was always cold in the closet, the floor freezing against my skin at night, but I grew used to it because I knew nothing else. Every now and then, my sister would put her fingers under the door and talk to me, and I latched on, starved for affection and attention of any sort. Her fingers brought me warmth, and her voice comforted me in my dark world. I loved listening to her voice. She tried to teach me to speak, but being unable to see her mouth to know how to pronounce the words, all I could do was try to mimic the sounds. My mentality was that of a deaf, dumb and blind child, so my thought process was completely off.

Sometimes my sister would slip a plate of mandarin oranges under the door. I had no idea what they were or what they looked like. I only knew they were the sweetest and most wonderful food in existence. Heavenly, in fact. Even now, in my fifties, mandarin oranges are my favorite thing in the world to eat. This one food was the single happy memory from that part of my childhood. I felt safe when my sister was around, yet she was never truly in my world.

Wanting so much to tell her how much her show of love meant to me, I couldn't form a single word, but for those brief moments, my heart was full.

To this day I still get a lump in my throat when I think of the secrets I was unable to share or express in words–dark secrets hidden from the world, secrets of things little girls and boys should never have to endure.

When I turned three, the light I was thrust into for short periods were for a different kind of bath time. Whenever the man living with my mother would bathe me, the water always hurt because I was usually abused first, both sexually and violently. I couldn't understand it. For so long there was no human contact other than physical abuse, and then there was this. During those times I cried out for help, but there were no words. There was no rescuer.

Mama yelled at me because I could not use the bathroom like a normal child. Again, I was never taught how. She decided the best way to teach me was by inserting a hose in my bottom, filling my stomach with water, then telling me to hold it until I reached the toilet to release. She did this many times and my bottom and stomach were always hurting. After these bouts of molestation, abuse, beatings and cleansing, sadness and exhaustion and the familiar darkness surrounding me would lull me to sleep. Every few days the process was repeated.

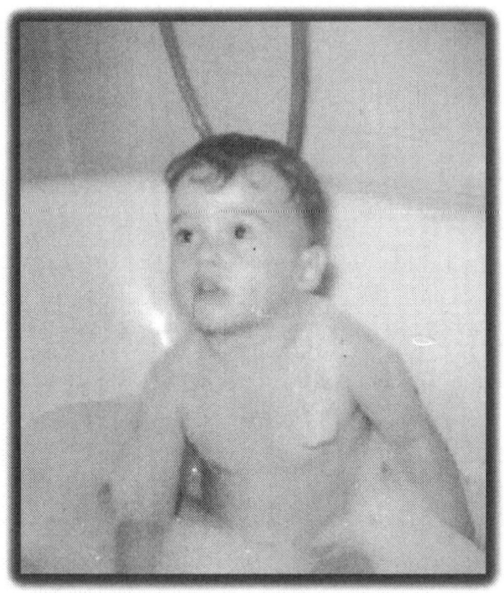

Every time I would press back into a corner in fear, my body shaking with the rattling of the door, my sister's little fingers were there petting mine and I made it through. Those were the only times I longed to get out of the closet. Because I knew she would never hit me or pull me by my feet and hurt me. She was the only living thing I trusted. Sometimes I would hear my sister crying for Mama to stop, and I wondered if some of the same things were being done to her. That hurt me just as much.

Then one day, I had grown too big for the broom closet. On that day my life changed.

* * *

My mother got her hair done on a regular basis and was friends with the hairdresser. Her name was Marian. Mama began taking me with her. For some reason the woman liked me. She was very kind and I always felt safe around her because she made me feel like I was the best little boy in the world. I really liked that feeling. What I felt at the salon was the polar opposite of what I felt at home where Mama would scream, "You're not James Bond 007, you're a doggy and a bad boy!" Then, because I would become frightened and soil my pants, she would again grab the hose and I was subjected to the same painful inner-cleansing, all in the name of potty training me.

One day after filling me with so much water that I passed out, I awakened in a place filled with light and people around me dressed in white. I had been taken to the hospital by my biological father. He had come back for one of his sparse visits. He was told that if I was abused again, I would be taken away. Listening, I lay in the hospital bed crying because I knew he would be leaving again and there would be no one there to rescue me.

My father always tried to protect me when he was there. Instead of taking me home, he asked others to watch over me, including Marian. This change was so drastic all I ever did was cry. The closet was the only life I knew and now I was being taken away from home and shuffled here and there to complete strangers.

Each time he left me with someone he told me, "This is your mommy for the weekend or this is your new daddy for the week, and you have got to be the best little boy in the world, which means you need to do whatever they say." Mama told me the same thing when she left me with someone. I remember crying, wanting to go back home to the closet because *that* was my home. I would do anything. I would work harder to be the best little boy in the world, if they would only let me go back home to my closet. And it was indeed *my* closet.

I went through weeks of this, and Mama and

Daddy continually fought over me. The last person I stayed with was Marian, or Aunt Marian as she was now called. During the two weeks I lived with her, I slowly opened up and began to trust her because she was so good to me. While I was there, she told me she was going to help me go to a good mommy and daddy. I just sat in the corner and cried. When she picked me up, I wrapped my arms around her neck and sobbed. I had never felt so much affection from someone. She whispered over and over that she would never let anything bad happen to me again.

In the comfort of her arms, we stood in front of the window staring out into the night, and at that moment, my conflicting thoughts calmed and all I could think about was I would never again be placed in the dark. None of those bad things would ever happen to me again.

Little did I know that words were being exchanged and a bargain was taking place.

I was being sold.

Yes, my new parents were acquiring me through black market means.

Mama and Daddy came to the beauty shop the

next day and told me I would be going to live with a new mommy and daddy. Aunt Marian had a sister who wanted to adopt a child and was willing to pay to do it. She and her husband purchased me and I now belonged to them. Again my unstable emotions swung and I cried because I did not want to go. I was used to the life I had. The closet was still normal to me, or rather my little brain again accepted it as normal, and my time with Aunt Marian was only a brief respite. I did not want to leave my world of 'stability'. Since living with Aunt Marian, I had learned to speak a few words, and did the best I could to ask my parents if they were mad at me for being a bad boy, and if that was the reason they didn't want me anymore. Of course, I couldn't form half the words and they never answered. Still, I pleaded the best I could for them to let me stay. I said I would be good if they would only keep me. My incoherent pleas went unheeded.

Mama dressed me in a little sailor suit and took a picture of me to send to the new family. Mama told me she and Daddy would be so happy for me, but things started clicking and I didn't believe it. How could a person who kept me locked in a closet and allowed other men to abuse me ever be happy about anything pertaining to me? I think if she was happy about anything, it was that she was getting rid of me. At the time I really couldn't tell how Daddy felt. I think he loved me, but maybe because he wouldn't always be there, he thought it was for the best.

I thought about the little girl who slid mandarin oranges under the door. I wondered what would happen to her. Would I ever see her again? I found out her name was Raylynn. My sister, Raylynn. She was always so good to me, and I would never get to know her. Years later I would find out that she and my brothers were farmed out to my grandparents.

That afternoon, Mama, Daddy and Raylynn took me to the airport. Standing at the edge of the tarmac, I looked out at the plane and had never in my life seen anything so big. Everything was overwhelming and all I wanted was to go back to my little broom closet where things were familiar. After all, it had been my comfort zone for two years, despite the times of terror.

Because the planes were so loud, my little body trembled and I wet my pants. This made Mama mad and she hit me, which felt completely normal. She then grabbed my head, looked down at me and said, "Jimmy, go get on that plane and don't leave your seat until your new mama and daddy come to the plane and get you. Now be a good boy and don't cry. And remember, you are going to have to be the best little boy in the world for someone to love you. You have to do what they tell you to do and listen to what they say."

I cried, holding to her, again incoherently pleading for her to let me stay, but she just pulled my hands away and push me forward. I had to walk across the tarmac to board the plane. When I reached the steps leading up to the door, I froze. I could hear Mama calling for me to go on up.

As the flight attendant descended the stairs to get me, I looked to my left and gasped. There stood an angel. No, I had never seen an angel before, but I knew I was looking at one. He was tall and had wings. To me, he was even bigger than the plane. When he looked at me, I felt like I knew him and he knew me. He then smiled at me and there were tears falling down his face. I immediately stopped crying, determined to not cry again after I got on the plane. No one would ever have a reason to give me away again because I would be a good boy. No one would ever beat me, hurt me or say I was bad ever again. No more ice cold baths or scalding hot baths, no more being filled with water by the hose.

I would be the best.

Smiling at the angel, I knew I would be okay. I wasn't afraid anymore. I did know him. I think I had always known him and was sure I would see him again.

The attendant took my hand and led me to my seat. Having been so isolated, touch was vital to me and I didn't want to let go of her hand. Smiling, she strapped me in and all I could do was sit back and accept things. I had no idea where I was going, just that I would be with a new mom and dad soon.

I also had no idea at the time that I had an additional angel looking out for me. Aunt Marian was sitting in the seat directly behind mine, seeing me safely to my destination.

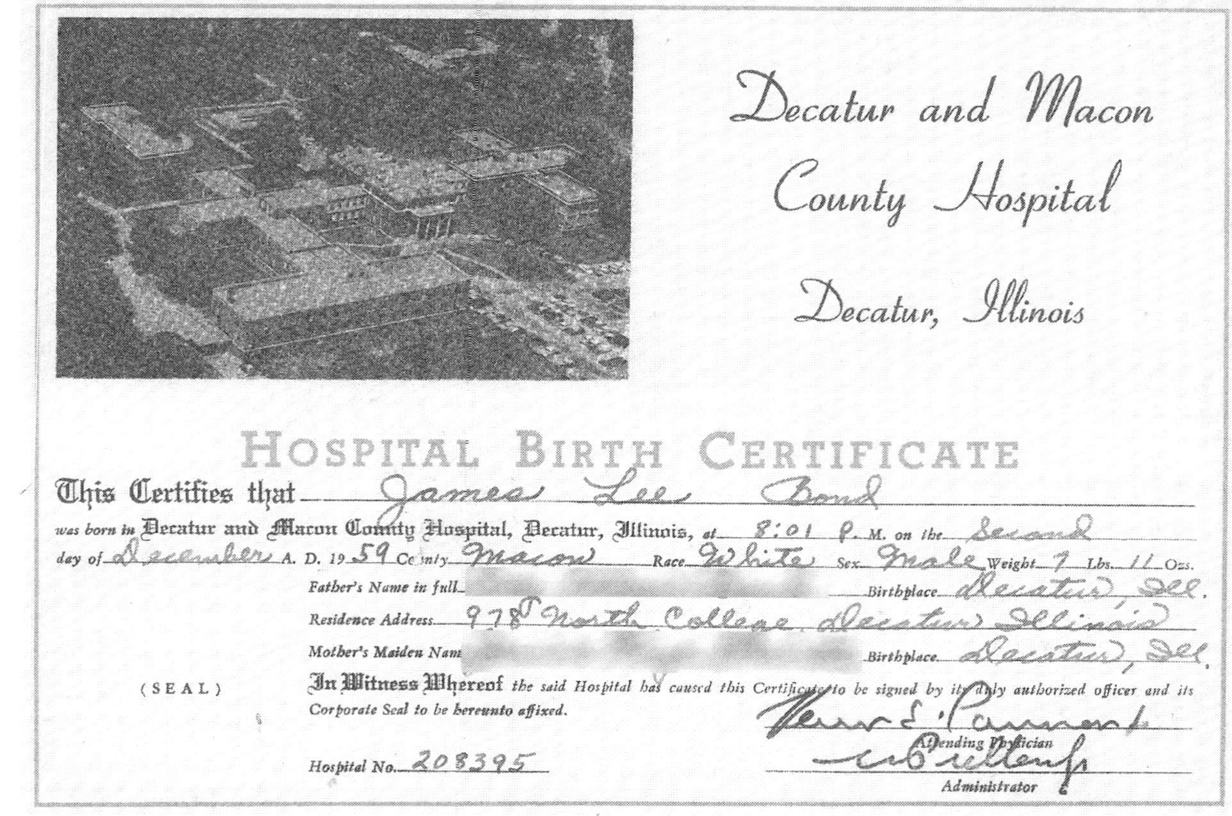

Decatur and Macon County Hospital

Decatur, Illinois

HOSPITAL BIRTH CERTIFICATE

This Certifies that James Lee Bond

was born in Decatur and Macon County Hospital, Decatur, Illinois, at 8:01 P. M. on the Second

day of December A. D. 1959 County Macon Race White Sex Male Weight 7 Lbs. 11 Ozs.

Father's Name in full [illegible] Birthplace Decatur, Ill.

Residence Address 978 North College, Decatur Illinois

Mother's Maiden Name [illegible] Birthplace Decatur, Ill.

(SEAL)

In Witness Whereof the said Hospital has caused this Certificate to be signed by its duly authorized officer and its Corporate Seal to be hereunto affixed.

Attending Physician

Hospital No. 208395

Administrator

Two

The New Family

Compton, California

My new parents changed my name to Jimmylee. Sadly, years later I would come to learn that they were only mine temporarily. I would also learn that some people treat their dogs better than their children, raising them under the "children should be neither seen or heard, but be perfect" motto. The family lived in a suburban community where everyone knew everyone and the houses were all very nice. My new home was pristine in cleanliness with nothing out of place, from the inside to the yards.

The family didn't know what to think of me. I was four years old and still wearing diapers. I didn't know how to use silverware properly, nor could I talk. I had to be taught all these things. It was definitely more than they bargained for. Mama was a stern woman with little patience. She wasn't an affectionate person, and in some ways, she reminded me of my biological mother. Daddy, however, was completely the opposite. He was soft-spoken and one of the kindest men I had ever met.

My first meal with them was tomato soup and grilled cheese sandwiches, which was easy for me to eat because I could just dip the sandwich in the soup. I didn't have to worry about how to use the silverware. In this way, the family was generous to me. There was also a daughter, so I had a new little sister. Her name was Tina. She was sweet and very trusting. We became close and were always together. We even took baths together for a while because I wasn't capable of bathing alone. This was comforting and made me less afraid of being hurt by the hose or other men. I was truly beginning to believe those things were no longer part of my life.

I was given new clothes and shoes to wear, as well as my own room. Daddy taught me to brush my teeth, comb my hair, and dress myself. He bought me toys and taught me how to play with them. Mama thought he was spoiling me, and maybe he was, but I know it was done out of love. He tried to make up for all I had been without.

Daddy wanted to teach me to trust because I really didn't know *how* to trust anyone. I remember him putting my sister and me on the roof of the house and having us jump off into his arms. The houses were built with low roofs back then, so an adult could stand and touch it. My sister always went first to show me it was okay while I stood back, shaking like crazy. But I figured if she could do it, I could too. He was strong and loving, and he never let me fall. So I started learning to trust him.

Daddy knew how to deal with me and was so kind. I knew he wanted a son–that he wanted *me*. I think it was hard for him knowing I had suffered so much abuse and neglect before coming to stay with them. He didn't know what type of abuse, but he knew some had been sexual, because of the times I acted out in front of him and Mama.

At those times, Daddy always talked with me and tried to help me work through things. He wasn't about to send me back to my biological family and made that clear each time I voiced my fear of that very thing.

I really needed that assurance, because after being with the family for a year, my biological mother contacted Mama and Daddy, asking for more money. My biological grandmother came to visit during this time as well and I was afraid she was coming to take me back. She said she only came to see how I was doing and make sure I was okay. She told me of my father's concern for me and how happy he was that I belonged to such a great family now. She even cried and told me how bad he felt about all the abuse, and how he wished he could have been there to stop it. The knowledge that he still thought of me brought me a small measure of comfort.

A month later, I had to stand in court and legally testify against my biological mother, which was really hard. I was only five at the time. The memory is a Polaroid snapshot in my mind. Mama and Daddy were soon able to legally adopt me. They changed my name for a new birth certificate. I was really theirs now and no one could take me away or make me go back. Looking back, I can see that I was just as adaptable as any other child. I adapted to this family soon enough, my innocence allowing me to eagerly accept whatever came with my membership in it, if only to truly belong somewhere.

* * *

Mama attempted to teach me how to talk better and how to write. She would pronounce words and I would repeat them. She then wrote the words and I attempted copy them. It was hard to learn because I had a difficult time understanding and didn't know how to respond or convey my feelings. In the past, I had been taught to act things out, but this behavior wasn't acceptable to Mama and she didn't know how to handle it. When she'd adopted my sister Tina before they got me, she had been pleased because Tina was smart and very normal. I wasn't. Mama had a lot of anger towards me, which came between her and Daddy. Daddy was a very significant part of my life because he was such a great human being. He loved me and was there to defend me as much as he could. He was a tree trimmer and was gone a lot, but when he was home, he spent a great deal of time with Tina and me.

Sometimes Daddy would come home and find me sitting in my closet. Though the smell and feel were different, I felt safe there. Whenever Mama was mean to me, I longed for that old broom closet again. There were nights when I would wake up, completely hysterical and Daddy would come and hold me. It was never Mama. It was always Daddy that did the soothing. He would rock me, telling me everything was going to be all right. This happened many times, the trauma crying, but he was always there.

I also learned many things from Tina–basic things like how to swing on a swing. I had never done that before and she taught me. Being outside during the day always hurt my eyes because I still wasn't used to it. I was so miserable from the light Daddy usually let me wear his sunglasses. Simple little things like that showed his love for me.

Tina filled a hole in my life that had been left by the absence of Raylynn. Only it went far deeper. I was able to see Tina's face every day, to truly know her. Still, there were times when the loss of the first sister brought me sadness. Then Tina would smile at me and the sadness faded.

Three

Discovered Talent

I was given a pair of tap shoes and enrolled in a tap dancing class. Tina was enrolled as well. I was the only boy in the class, but I picked it up immediately. It was like I was born to tap. I think the ability started when I was locked in the closet. Sitting in the dark, I used to make a popping sound with my mouth. Since I didn't know how to speak, the sound kept me company, like talking to myself without words. The popping soon developed a rhythm and the sound embedded itself in me, which is why tap came so easily. I made the popping sound while I tapped and it guided me, helping me to dance in synch. The teacher was completely blown away by my skills. Though I still couldn't talk well, I could understand her instructions and was able to follow her lead. And I nailed every routine. Tap dancing brought me a joy that could not be expressed in words. I felt free when I danced, an undefined happiness that I latched on to and held on for dear life. When I danced, all the cares and troubles of my little world went away.

After many, many classes, my parents had me audition for Disney. The people I auditioned for liked what they saw and had me perform some numbers with groups of children. I was always placed up front. They told my mother they had to have me up front and she couldn't understand why Tina couldn't be up front, too. They said that though she was good, she wasn't as good as I was, which brought a little animosity from my mother toward me and my gift of dance. But I still tried to make her happy by being the best tap dancer I could be.

Soon we were participating in the Disneyland parades. We would dance and sing, our main number being, *Tiny Little Troopers.* We began traveling, and for the next while, we were performing all over. Disney children practiced anywhere from twelve to sixteen hours a day and we were always exhausted, but we did it without complaint. We were never able to make friends or get to know the other kids much because there was never time, but our daily lives mirrored one another.

Tina and I were even enrolled in roller skating and did couples skating. We had so much fun together and I enjoyed just being with her, because she was everything I wanted to be. Life was good and I was happy. I had a family, I had my tap dancing and my very own shoes–something I became very attached to. I was unable to form many attachments, but my tap shoes meant the world to me. Little did I know my world was about to be shaken up yet again.

Four

Uncle Arthur

Getting to know Mama and Daddy's family, I gravitated more toward Daddy's because they were so kind to me. They lived in a small southern Baptist community and were good people. They knew about the life I'd come from and treated me well. They were open with their affections and made every effort to show me I was loved.

Daddy's father was disabled and in a wheelchair. He took me fishing and taught me how to bait the hook. Daddy would sit on the porch watching and laughing as Granddaddy let me push him in his wheelchair and ride on the back. He put up with so many of my antics because he knew doing these things made me happy, which made him happy. He was very patient with me and I grew to love him as much as I loved my dad. I felt safe with them because their love was unconditional.

But Mama's family was different. I didn't enjoy going to see them at all because they were not so patient and I was constantly trying to prove myself. And at my age, with my mental capabilities, that was pretty hard. The exceptions were Mama's mother and father. They were good to me and I liked them a lot. Other than that, the family was far more uppity and thought highly of themselves.

During one of these visits to Mama's parents' home, I met Mama's brother, and he was everything I thought I'd escaped.

He was Satan incarnate.

Uncle Arthur knew an easy target when he saw it. Armed with knowledge of my life and what I'd been through before coming to the family, he immediately began sexually abusing me.

The first day I met him, Uncle Arthur told me to take a walk with him. He took me out to his father's barn. Inside were chicken pens. The barn was large and the floor was covered in straw and wood chip shavings, the smell of animals thick in the air. There were two separate coops–one for the hens, the other for fighting roosters. They were huge, easily the biggest birds I had ever seen, and the flapping wings made them look even bigger. Of course, when you're a kid, everything looks bigger.

He made me stand in one spot, telling me not to move. As I stood trembling, he held one of the large flapping roosters to my face, running the sharp claws over my skin. Threatening me, he said, "You see this? If you don't do what I tell you, I will kill your daddy."

I told him I would do anything if he would not hurt Daddy. I even said he could hurt Mama if he would just leave my daddy alone. He knew he had me then, because he knew how much I loved Daddy. He let the rooster's claws touch my skin again. He then applied the little knives that were normally on the rooster's feet to his own fingers and ran them up and down my skin, repeating the threat. Again, I promised I would do what he wanted. Smiling an evil smile I would forever associate with him, he put the rooster back in the pen, then pulled me behind the cages and raped me.

Sobbing, all I could do was close my eyes and try to shut out the pain. When I cried out, he covered my mouth with his hand. My mind soon shifted and I was once again James Lee Bond, back in the dark, pungent closet, shut away from the rest of the world.

* * *

After that, I was always afraid for Daddy, always hoping my uncle would keep his promise. One day, Uncle Arthur had even managed to hold a knife up to my father's neck in a joking manner during one of the visits, and threatened to kill him. Daddy said to go ahead. I walked in on this situation, and since I was already terrified, I didn't know what was happening. All I knew was he would truly kill Daddy if I ever said anything. And that is exactly what he wanted. My fate with him was sealed.

Because of my uncle, I was learning to talk more. He taught me words of submission, and each time we went for a visit, the first thing I would say to him was,

"I'll do anything." He would then take me to the back of the barn and abuse me. I started begging Mama not to take me, but she made me go anyway. Each time I went, I dreaded that old building more than any other place on the farm. I had nightmares about the barn, about Uncle Arthur, and the rooster. I didn't think anything could be worse.

But I was wrong.

Soon the ritual abuse began and there was a new dreaded place.

One day Mama left me at my grandparent's place for the day. Uncle Arthur took me out into the family's large orange grove. He brought a chicken and a knife. When we reached an area deep within the trees, he told me to stand still while he cut the head from the chicken. Having finished, he pulled my clothes off, rubbed the blood all over my body, then called on Satan to inhabit his own body before pinning me down and molesting me. He ran the rooster knives all over me. I was so frightened and in so much pain, I cried out, but no one came to rescue me. I cried so much, my nose was stopped up and I couldn't breathe, not just from pain, but fear. I was completely at Uncle Arthur's mercy, my fate in his hands.

Soon his friends became involved in the rituals. They called the ceremony 'cleansing me with the blood.' Satan was constantly called upon during these 'ceremonies.' The blood was slimy and seemed to burn as they spread it all over me, including in my groin and other private areas. The sensation was worse than the feel of my own waste on my skin while living in the closet, and my mind always seemed to split in two until they finished. The men would take turns, and by the time they were done, I always in so much pain I could barely walk.

My cousins knew about the rituals because they would hose the blood off me afterward. No one ever said anything and I often wondered if the same things were being done to them.

Each time I returned home, I would go to the closet and curl into a ball, wanting no one to touch me. I couldn't bear for anyone to get close. Then I would get into bed and pray for the angel to come and take me away. He may have come, I'm not sure. But he never took me away. There was always more of the same.

The rituals were just another prelude of things to come.

Five

Unwanted House Guest

Three years later.

Uncle Arthur came to stay with us and I was told I had to share my room with him. Later I would come to learn more about him; he'd been married a couple of times before, but because of his mood swings, both wives left him. Maybe they realized how sick and disturbed he was and got out while they could. In that way, they were lucky. They rid themselves of him, unknowingly leaving a little boy to suffer the disgusting aftermath left in their wake.

My grandparents were happy to have him living with us because they were tired of dealing with him, too. Daddy knew I didn't like Uncle Arthur, but because of Mama, there was nothing he could do. She basically wore the pants in the family. I begged her to not make me share my room, but as usual, I was ignored. So my nights were filled with abuse. He never left me alone and life was even worse. Even with the satanic ritual abuse, I always had a week before I was taken back there again. Now there was no break. Again, I thought nothing could be worse.

Then I was thrust into a completely different world.

My uncle started taking me with him to adult bookstores where I was forced to have sex with men in a back room. To get me relaxed and more malleable the first time, he gave me little white cross-top speed pills and told me they were vitamins and would help me. They became a part of each trip there.

Uncle Arthur always told Mama and Daddy he was taking me out for a while. They never had a clue that I was being used by him and other strange men at the adult bookstore, a place you are supposed to be eighteen to even get into. Whenever Tina asked where I was going, I lied because I was forbidden to tell her, and I was afraid he would hurt her. I couldn't let that happen.

He took me there several times a week, and despite all of my hoping that I wouldn't be touched, there were always men waiting. Many nights I would cry myself to sleep, longing for some peace, longing to be left alone. Then Uncle Arthur would come in and my hopes were shattered. Soon, the hope began to fade and I just dealt with it. This was my life. It was a reality that I couldn't wish away no matter how hard I tried.

Sadly, it slowly became normal to me.

Six

The Arcade

I sometimes experienced flashbacks. Doctors didn't know exactly where I was mentally, physically or emotionally, and I sometimes had such temper tantrums, it was hard to know what to do. It was impossible for me to explain why I didn't want to be touched, and why certain smells even set me off. At times those moments were terrifying, not only for me, but those around me. I was considered disturbed and problematic. And neither were my fault.

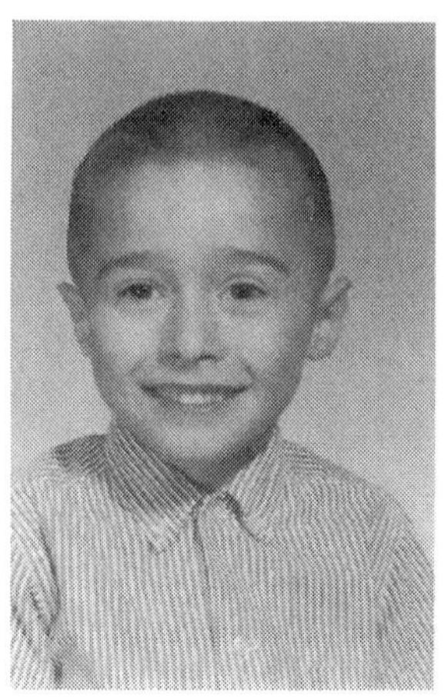

At ten years old, I was in the fourth grade for the second time, and not only was I having problems learning, I was still learning to write Jimmylee and not James Bond 007. I was also inclined to try and hold hands with other boys. I was so messed up mentally and emotionally, yet all my teachers stated on my report cards that I lacked self-confidence. I was ten with the mentality of an six year old, and they thought I lacked *self-confidence.* They complained about me not having the ability to sit quietly. My constant need to go to the bathroom was also disruptive. Of course, the bathroom breaks were caused by the abuse–the sexual, as well as the lingering effects of the forced enemas from before. But I couldn't tell anyone.

In school, I used red a lot when coloring. The teacher asked me one day why I used it so much and I replied, "Because that is the color that comes out of me." I am sure she thought I meant the color of blood when I bled, but she had no idea how literal that was.

Mama was embarrassed by me. She was also angry and verbally abusive whenever my teacher contacted her. It was killing her that I wasn't normal, that I wasn't going out and doing things like other boys, that I wasn't learning like a normal child my age. I always played with girls instead of boys because I felt more comfortable. Because of this, I endured the usual name calling, some names worse than others, though it didn't occur to me at the time.

Mama soon joined the PTA and became more involved with the school to keep a closer eye on what I was doing. I had begun acting out sexually in school as well, and this wouldn't do at all.

Daddy literally stopped me in the act one day and asked me, "Why are you doing this, son?"

I said, "I do this to make you happy, so you will

love me." This is what I had been taught, how I had been groomed by my biological mother and her boyfriends to think. Doing this made me *the best little boy in the world.*

But this time I was afraid, because the way Daddy asked this and looked at me made me realize that what I was doing wasn't making him happy. It was making him sad. This was an eye opener and helped me to finally stop.

* * *

During that year, I began going to play pinball at the bowling alley with other children from school. A few of the parents would carpool. I'd never been in a bowling alley before or anywhere near a pinball game. It was the most exciting thing that had ever happened to me. The man who owned the place said he would let me play all I wanted for free.

In exchange for doing what he wanted.

I soon discovered the bowling alley was a facade for other things. While the adults bowled, I was taken into a back room with other boys my age where we were told to undress and perform sexual acts with each other. These acts were always photographed or filmed.

The other boys seemed just as used to being touched as I was.

I was told to keep this secret, and as long as I did whatever the owner said, I could play all the pinball and other games I wanted. Since it didn't involve anyone hurting me, the arrangement sounded ideal. This was my introduction into the world of pornography. I still had no idea how terribly wrong and sick this all was.

My whole life now consisted of sex–performing the acts in front of a camera during the week, suffering its abuse at the hand of my uncle at night–as well as a couple of the male neighbors who recently discovered what I could do–and visits to the adult bookstore on various weekends. I would take the arcade over the latter three any day.

ACHIEVEMENT RECORD FOR THIS REPORT PERIOD

PUPIL Jimmy Grubbs

SCHOOL Henry TEACHER Strauch

Present Grade 4th ~~Promoted to~~ Recommended for 4th

Growth Report for 1969-70 (School Year) ______ (First Semester) X (Second Semester)

Jimmy finds almost all fourth grade work too difficult. Although he reads orally with some fluency, most of the meaning escapes him. In math, he has been working in a third grade book most of the year.

It is so important for a child to feel successful in his work. With success, he can develop self-confidence.

Every child has his own rate of mental growth and it is not necessarily related to his physical growth or chronological age. I feel certain that next year Jimmy will be more ready for fourth grade work and will have a better chance to achieve success.

Seven

Fed Up

Uncle Arthur was relentless in his taunting and abuse, and the trips to the adult bookstore hadn't slowed.

One day I got so tired of it that I finally told Mama what he was doing to me. I didn't tell Daddy because I didn't want anything to happen to him. I begged her not to tell anyone because he would kill Daddy. Later in life I would learn that this was the standard manipulating procedure for abusers.

Mama was surprised at how well I was now

talking. I told her Uncle Arthur had been teaching me that, and many other things. I told her in detail what those things were, and she didn't believe me. She said I was making it all up and told me to never say anything to anyone, and that if I did, I would no longer be living with them.

"Please don't," I pleaded. "Where will I go? No one will want me."

"Oh, you won't ever have a problem finding a home," she told me. "Because you're a pretty little boy and you're talented. As long as you're a good boy, everyone will want you."

"Please don't get rid of me," I continued to beg. "Don't give me away. I'll be good, I promise."

Taking my arm, she pulled me out to the garage. I knew what was coming. Beatings in the garage were nothing new. This area of the house was as familiar to me as the old broom closet. Only in the garage, my screams couldn't be camouflaged.

Grabbing the cord she always used, she began to beat me, saying over and over, "You had better not tell anyone. Not a word, do you hear me? Not one word! I promise you if you tell anyone, you will be gone."

* * *

One of my teachers began to notice my growing gravitation toward the boys in my class. She also started noticing bloodstains on the back of my pants. Finally pulling me aside, she asked me about it. I told her I fell and that I would be in trouble because I wasn't allowed to get my clothes dirty. She asked me about other problems I had been having, like soiling myself and having to go to the bathroom all the time. She even noticed small amounts of blood on me before but hadn't said anything.

I finally told her I was gay. I had heard the word used so much by other kids in reference to me, I knew what it meant. I also told her about Uncle Arthur and what he was doing to me. She asked for specifics and I told her everything. I shared how I would pretend I was James Bond 007, which threw her for a loop. She had no clue how that name connected to my past.

Because homosexuality was considered a mental illness in the sixties, the teacher immediately sent me to the principal's office and told him they needed to call my parents and let them know what was going on. I knew I shouldn't have told her and I was afraid, because I also knew what the consequences would be. By telling her this, I had done something wrong and would be punished for it.

Mama came to the school, spoke with the teacher and the principal, made excuses, and said she would take me to the doctor. Of course, this was completely for show. When you are raised in a family with money, anything can be covered up. It can pay for a clean bill of health, as well as a psychiatric evaluation suggesting that your son be put in special education because he is mentally challenged and needs extra help.

Money can also buy silence. So the abuse didn't stop, and I wound up sitting in a classroom full of drooling children stacking blocks and coloring. I had no idea where I fit in. Not that I ever did.

* * *

A day dawned when I'd finally had it. I was sick of it all, and I was done sharing my room with my sick uncle. I was finished being scared to death, listening to him talk about evil spirits coming down and inhabiting his body, giving him power to do the things he did to me. I once briefly believed he was a man of God because he had my thoughts so twisted, but I knew now that there was absolutely nothing of God in him. It was completely the opposite. Unwilling to deal with his manipulation any longer, I learned how to reverse the roles.

I had a little Buddha I'd gotten from my biological grandmother. That little statue was my ticket to a big change.

"You see this Buddha?" I said, holding it up to him one day. "It's possessed and it sees you. It sees everything." Then I placed the statue on the table by my bed, completely freaking him out. Since he was already a psychotic heretic, that wasn't hard to do. He completely believed me. He immediately told Mama and she asked me why I told him that.

"Because he's crazy," I told her. "And why is he still in my room? I want him out of there. I hate him and I want him dead." Then of course, she got mad and once again I was beaten, but I didn't care. I'd had it with Uncle Arthur.

Afterward, I ranted at her, saying, "You just don't believe anything I say."

To which she replied, "You go and apologize to

your uncle."

"I won't, and I'm not sorry."

I had braces at the time, so when she grabbed my face and squeezed my cheeks hard, it was excruciating. But I was not about to apologize, no matter what she did to me.

She said, "You think that's your room? You think anything we've bought you is yours? Well, it's not. You were used shoes when we bought you and you still are."

"What do you mean?" I asked, not understanding.

"I mean we bought you second hand. All of this stuff was done to you long before you came to us. Uncle Arthur didn't do it, it was already done."

"Why are you saying this?"

"Because you were gay before you came to us. Uncle Arthur had nothing to do with it."

"But he does stuff to me all the time. He puts rooster blood on me and calls down Satan when he does it. He hurts me. He makes me let other men do it, too."

Glaring at me a final time, she repeats, "You

were used shoes when you came, end of discussion. You will never mention this again."

* * *

After months of retaliating with the Buddha threat, Uncle Arthur slowly began to lose his sanity. Part of it was due to all the other crazy things he had, and was still doing in his life. He would soon check in to a mental health facility and be in and out of the place for the rest of my childhood.

Eight

Struggling Through

Mama and Uncle Arthur were two very deceiving people, and there was so much kept from Daddy. Still, he could see how much I was struggling. Watching me grow more miserable with each passing day, he finally asked me if I wanted to go and stay with my aunt and uncle for the summer and get away for a while. I quickly said yes.

My aunt and uncle lived on a potato farm and life was quite different there. For one thing, I got to keep my clothes on and no one touched me or tried to hurt me in any way. I actually got to be a kid. I was amazed that the two sides of the family could be so different and I quickly bonded with the couple. Aunt Ellen always told me I was her favorite nephew, and she spoiled me the entire time I was there. She showered me with a mother's love and took care of me, something no woman had ever done before. But she and Uncle Peter thought Mama was a wonderful mother and never saw her as she really was. Mama had the entire family on both sides fooled, and it was pointless to say anything negative about her, so I didn't. I spent the time roaming around the farm, talking to the animals, and helping my aunt and uncle with whatever needed to be done. They were appreciative of every effort I made. My time with them was special, one that I would never forget.

* * *

When I finally returned home, I enrolled in fifth grade and life became worse. Not only was my uncle still at me, but now I was being approached by male teachers and kept after school for more molestation. I became so mentally messed up, I finally went to Daddy one day and said, "Something is wrong with me. I like the boys in school instead of the girls."

"What do you mean?" he asked.

"They say I'm gay because I want to hold hands with boys and kiss them like you and Mama do. There's something wrong with me."

I could tell this was hard for him to hear, but he didn't get mad or angry. He was such a patient man. He simply said, "We're going to kneel beside the bed and pray."

So we prayed, and I will never forget what I felt kneeling beside my dad as he prayed for me. No one had ever done that before. He prayed that God would protect me. Daddy also asked God to help me learn to trust him and know that I could tell him anything. Afterward, he hugged me and told me I was a good son and I could talk to him about anything I wanted. He promised to always listen.

Mama was jealous of my relationship with Daddy because he was always such a happy person and showed me so much love. She knew I trusted him and loved him more than anyone else. But she could never see that Daddy *earned* my love. She didn't.

* * *

By the time I reached the sixth grade, I'd had enough of home and school. The only way I even passed to the sixth grade was by allowing the teachers to do whatever they wanted to me after school. No one ever knew what went on behind those closed classroom doors. I couldn't do the schoolwork. I couldn't read or write well, so I didn't even *understand* the work. And Mama was not going to have me repeat the fifth grade again. Looking back, I am sure she knew what was happening after school. She just let it happen.

At the end of that school year, I was tired of being around Mama and did the only thing I knew to do.

I ran away.

At twelve years old, I hopped a bus and left for the summer.

Nine

San Diego

I took a bus to San Diego. These days that kind of thing would be unheard of, not to mention impossible. But life was very different then. I had no idea where I was going, only that I was getting away from home and escaping a life of being used for everyone else' gratification.

When I got off the bus, I met a man who would continue my education in the world of sex and pornography. He said his name was Jim, and as I got to know him, I shared things about myself, including all the molestation and abuse. I specified that my father had never touched me in that way, and from him I received nothing but a father's love. I refused to ever have anyone think badly of him.

Ever.

Getting into Jim's blue van, we went to his very nice home where he told me I would be taken care of for the summer. Before I knew it, he was introducing me to other boys–some my age, some older–and had me shooting videos with them. He'd also met these young men at various bus stops. They traveled from different parts of California, many of them coming from situations similar to mine.

Jim took us to Hollywood and my eyes grew as big as saucers. I couldn't believe I was actually there, the city of the movie stars. I took mental snapshots of everything I saw.

He had a standing room at the Beverly Wilshire Hotel. It was reserved for only one purpose: for men to come and photograph young boys in sexual acts.

This would be my first paying job. For the entire time I was in San Diego, Jim kept me working in kiddie porn. I had money, clothes, everything I wanted. We traveled out to Catalina Island as well. While there, we stayed in mansions, ate great food, and met many influential people. I had no idea just how influential these people were, I only knew they were important and rich. I unknowingly made connections, and did photos and videos for the whole summer.

* * *

I returned home at the start of junior high, but kept in contact with Jim. I went back to San Diego for the next two summers and started working a little for an escort service that specifically employed kids under eighteen. It was different than anything I'd done previously. I went through all the grooming and training, learning how to be all thing to all clients. I had many clients and was always booked. I was usually taken to meet the man, and then told to do whatever he requested, which wasn't anything out of the ordinary, at least, nothing I hadn't already done before going to California in the first place. Both summers were full and I made great money.

Mama never seemed to care that her young son was catching a bus to San Diego, but to keep Daddy from worrying, I lied and said I was working at a drive-in burger place there, and since the owner was part of the pornography ring, he had no problem vouching for me working there.

My interactions with Uncle Arthur were getting more intense because I now stood up to him, telling him that I would kill him before he killed Daddy. I was no longer afraid and my threats kind of freaked him out. I told him about Jim and many other friends I was involved with, saying that I could have him killed whenever I wanted. In retaliation, he did everything he could to make me look bad in the eyes of their side of the family and I was basically blacklisted. As far as they were concerned, there was nothing redeeming about me.

On one visit to Mama's parent's home, I solidified that opinion. I became so angry over everything Uncle Arthur had ever done to me I went to the coops and killed all the fighting roosters. My grandfather was livid because they were a big moneymaker for him. Even though I was sorry for hurting him that way, I couldn't help the satisfaction I felt when it was done. For too many nights, those birds had haunted my dreams. I was no longer afraid of the roosters or Uncle Arthur, or anything. Sure, they thought I was even more mentally imbalanced, but that no longer mattered to me, either.

I left again, but this time Jim took me to Ventura, California where I did more videos. When I got back, Mama had found some of my headshots and asked who took them. I told her they were taken by an agency in Ventura. She immediately showed them to Daddy and he asked, "Who would do this?"

"They were taken by a modeling agency in Ventura so they can have each kid's picture on file for jobs." I wasn't lying, I just didn't tell them what kind of jobs they were.

They both said the pictures were incredible. Daddy wanted to know who owned the cars in the photos. I was photographed leaning against various expensive vehicles. I told him they belonged to some of the employers. He believed me and nothing else was said.

My relationship with Tina became strained, not only because I was leaving so much, but because she thought I was abandoning her. Mama definitely had something to do with this, and I would find out later that she'd been slowing poisoning my sister's thoughts and trying to turn her against me. Tina had no idea what I had gone through for so many years and couldn't understand that the trips were my escape from the hell I had lived in for so long. I'd leaned on her a great deal and I knew I couldn't do that anymore. She was the reason I stayed in school and tried so hard to be good at everything. I wanted to be like her, because she was everything that was good in my life. Mama knew this and did what she could to ruin our relationship. I think she started this process from the very beginning. Years later I would come to understand just how much she truly hated me.

* * *

My parents started having major marital problems. They argued almost every day and I knew it was only a matter of time before something happened. I never told Daddy what I endured, and to this day, he still doesn't know. I've never wanted him to.

Through it all, life went on.

Ten

New Profession

The year I turned fifteen, I started working for *California's Finest* at night and went to school during the day. Every client using this escort service was into sleeping with children and paid well for it. Since the jobs were by the hour, I worked a few hours each week in the evenings, managing to keep it from Mama and Daddy. I was never seen by anyone I knew. Not that I really worried about it. Daddy wouldn't have believed it anyway, and Mama wouldn't have cared, unless, of course, it affected her personally.

I began to make a lot of new discoveries that year–none of them ones that I should have been making. One day I met some people at a gay bar located across the street from the driving school. Daddy dropped me off at the school, and after my class, I walked over. I shouldn't have even been allowed to enter, but since it wasn't your average bar, it didn't matter. After talking with a few guys a bit, they invited me to go with them to Laguna Beach that weekend. It was an adult nude beach. I wanted to go but knew I needed to come up with a plan. When Daddy came to get me, I told him the instructor at the driving school was treating the students to a day at the beach that Saturday and he would give me a ride home. Seeing how excited I was about it, he said I could go.

Daddy dropped me off at the school on Saturday morning and asked me if I would be okay. I assured him I would and he left. The whole day was a strange experience. Everyone drank alcohol, and though I had no interest in it, I enjoyed playing beach ball and made a lot of friends. Through these friends, I gained connections that led me to work in the adult porn industry.

I traveled all over California and Catalina Island, making films and escorting. This and school were my entire life. And by the time I was a junior in high school, I was a seasoned professional in the adult industry. This is not said with pride or boasting, it was just a fact.

* * *

During my senior year, I got a legitimate modeling job for Sears and JC. Penny as an underwear model. In addition, I was escorting and making movies, so I was able to show Daddy legitimate work and still make good money. Sears and Penny paid nowhere near what the porn industry did. And through the escort services, particularly the *Male Order Bride* service, I gained some very influential and high standing clients. The names were numerous and will forever stay buried in my memory. While working for this service, I traveled extensively–I told Daddy they were modeling gigs– and gained more knowledge of the adult world. I was paid to be a temporary companion and would live with a client for a few weeks. Some of the clients became long-term friends and helped to further my career. Some were clothing designers, which got me into runway modeling. Among those were Ocean Pacific and Dolphin Sun Wear. I really loved doing runway, and having become disillusioned with *Male Order Brides,* I left the service and did more legitimate modeling.

My appearance on the covers of gay magazines increased. Since I wasn't eighteen yet, I used a fake ID I had acquired with a fake birth certificate made for me by a neighbor. Thinking about it now, it amazes me how depraved people can be, but I didn't think anything of it then.

As far as school went, things were about the same with one exception. I made the cheer leading squad with Tina and was the mascot. Daddy told me that if I was going to do it, I needed to be the best mascot they'd ever had. Taking his words to heart, I practiced and practiced, then won the state competition at Pepperdine University. It was a wonderful accomplishment for me and I'll always treasure that memory.

A week later while sitting at the dinner table, Mama told Daddy she wanted a divorce. Completely shocked, I was angry at her and wondered how she could do that to Daddy. Then she informed us that she would be taking Tina with her and that I was staying with him. Saying nothing, he got up and left. I then turned to her and said, "So, is Daddy a pair of used shoes now, too?" She immediately slapped me, which I'd expected, but it didn't stop me. "You can break up this family, but you will never come between me and my dad."

She quickly replied, "He never was your dad. You've had many dads, so you don't really have any parents. The best thing you can do is leave this family and never come back. You have shamed us and you are an embarrassment to all of us, including your sister. She has been embarrassed by you in school and is tired of you. And so am I. That's why she agreed to come with me."

I wished Tina had been there so I could ask her if this was true, but since she'd been acting so different to me lately, I believed Mama's words. Saying nothing else, I got up and went to my room. I just sat and cried, unable to believe Mama could be so cruel. I don't know why, because she had always been cruel to me and that would never change. I should have been happy she was leaving, but her taking Tina made it painful. At that moment, I didn't know where I would go or what I would do. I felt so misplaced and could sense myself regressing a little. James Bond was there just below the surface. For some reason, I remembered the angel at the plane again. I hadn't thought of him in a while, but I really needed him at that moment. I found myself praying for the angel to help keep my family together because I needed them. As bad as it was, having them together was the only stable thing in my life, even as distorted as my view of stability was.

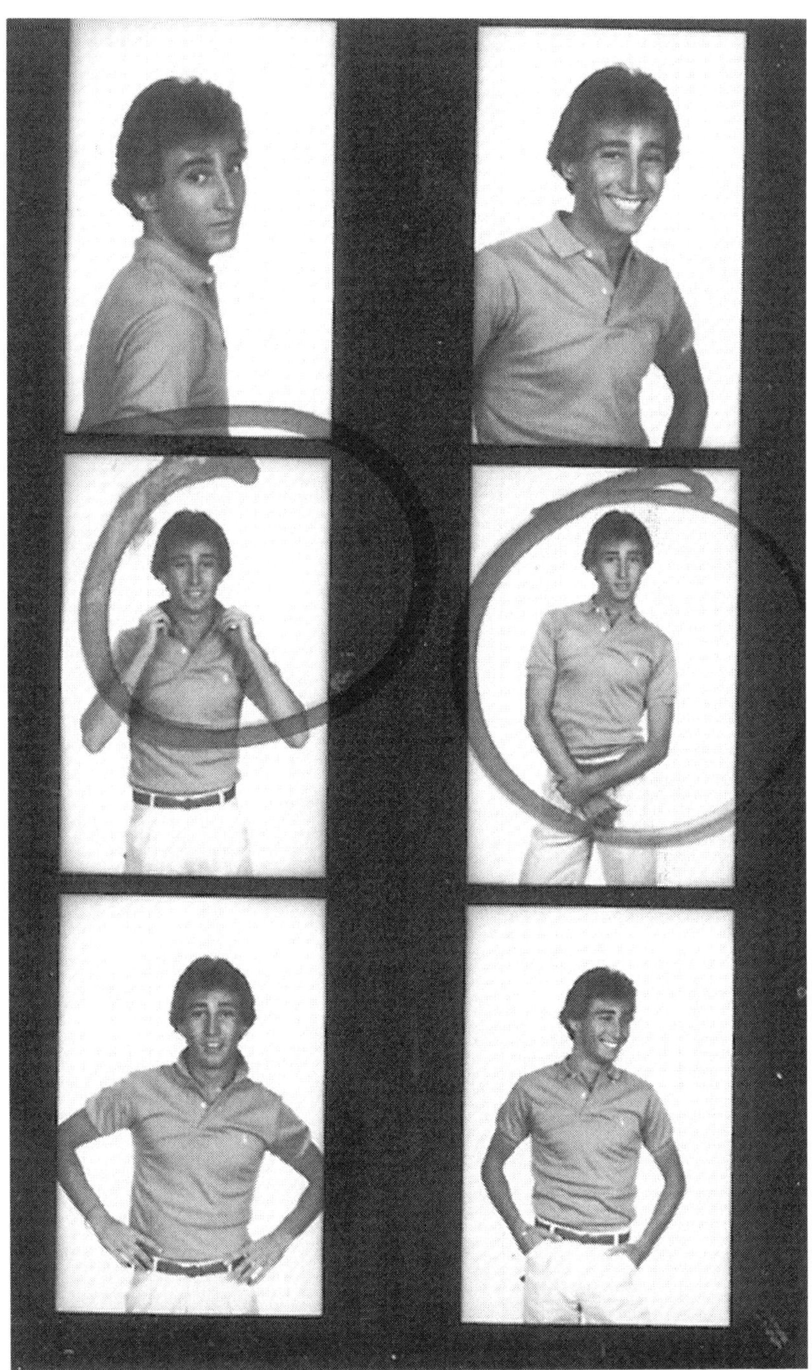

Eleven

A Different Kind of Pain

After Mama moved out, I stayed with Daddy for a while and continued to model and do videos. Not knowing then how many people those videos would reach–and are still reaching even now–I will forever be ashamed. I regret doing them, because I will never escape knowing they are out there. Back then, it never occurred to me to think of the future. That *was* my future.

Daddy finally told me one day that he was getting married again. The woman was nice, but I worried that she would take my father away from me. He was the only person I had left in the world and I couldn't afford to lose him, too. He did his best to assure me that would never happen, and his new wife was nothing but kind to me, showing me more love than Mama ever did. Still, they had a new life of their own, which meant it was time to be on my own. Problem was, I knew no other life than the one I was living.

* * *

I finally moved to Los Angeles. While there, I met up with a dangerous and affluent Italian man with his own mafia circle. I met Jonah through *Male Order Brides* and was now working for an escort service he ran. I wasn't really interested in steady companionship, but he was attractive and very nice to me. He bought me clothes, took me traveling, and made sure I had whatever I needed. It was an ideal situation.

In the beginning.

Ours turned into a two-year volatile relationship. Jonah was very controlling and violent. He went with me everywhere. Except for when I was with clients, I never went anywhere alone.

If I went into the grocery store, he would sit out in the car with a pair of binoculars, watching me to see if I was flirting with the checker. Then he would take me home and beat me. The slightest little thing would set him off. If I even smiled at another man, I was beaten, sometimes so brutally, I ended up in the emergency room. The man's mother and two sisters feared for my life. They finally pulled me aside one day and said we were going to leave. Otherwise I would be killed.

"You've got to get away from here, Jimmy," Penny, his mother, told me. "Because he's not going to let you go. You are basically supporting him. He makes enough money off you to pay for his entire lifestyle. If you stay any longer, you'll wind up dead."

"But why would you all leave?" I asked Kim, one of the sisters.

"Because we're afraid, too. Our brother and his people are dangerous."

And Paula added, "How do you think we lost our father?"

That did it for me. So in the middle of the night, they helped me escape to Portland, Oregon. We got an apartment and settled in the city.

I soon went to work for another escort service, but before long, restlessness hit. I don't know why I did it, but I flew to Phoenix a few times, and from there took a flight back to California to the man I'd just escaped from. It was like I was so connected and conditioned, I couldn't stay away. I didn't tell Jonah's mother and sisters because I knew they would be angry, and I didn't want him to discover where we lived. That is the reason I flew out of Phoenix.

The last time I went, I met him *in* Phoenix. During this meeting, I was intimately roughed up more than ever before, and then beaten so badly, he literally knocked me out. I lost a tooth in the process.

When Jonah dropped me off at the airport, I was so physically battered and out of it, I couldn't even remember the trip home. However, this final trip knocked some sense into me, *literally*! And I knew things would have to change.

Twelve

The Wedding

I went back to Compton for Tina's wedding. She was marrying a guy we met one night at a dance club and had become good friends with. Dan was a nice guy and I figured they would be happy together.

Though it was great to see Tina, the visit was strained and short. She did not ask me to be in the wedding party, nor be involved in any way, so I was just a guest like everyone else.

That really hurt.

I sat next to Grandma Grubbs and she was

happy to see me. I really missed her and was looking forward to visiting with her. Grandpa had passed away from cancer a few years before and I missed him as well.

Mama and her family sat on the other side of the church and wouldn't even acknowledge me. The hatred in her eyes hadn't dimmed at all. But Grandma Parker was glad to see me. Grandpa Parker wasn't able to make it, so Grandma was also flying solo that day.

Despite the piercing stares and whispers directed at me from many in the congregation–I was used to being gossiped about–the ceremony was very nice and Tina was beautiful, but the distance between us was as vast as the Grand Canyon. She still didn't know about my life or what I did for a living. No one did. They only knew I'd disappeared. As far as the family was concerned, I cared about no one but myself, and there was nothing I could do or say to change it.

Mama made sure of that.

Because it was Tina's wedding day, I wasn't able to talk with her much, just a few words here and there. But I don't think it would have made a difference if the situation had been different. Mama had sown the seeds of destruction between us and I wasn't sure my relationship with Tina would ever bear fruit again.

I had a good visit with both grandmothers and was assured of their love. I didn't know when I would see either of them again and I would miss them both. And as I readied myself to leave–there was no point in me staying any longer just to be ignored–Mama was inclined to give me one last parting crippling blast.

"Jimmy, I don't know why you came. Nobody wanted you here. That's why Tina didn't ask you to be in the wedding. You're still an embarrassment. Always have been and always will be. I told you before, the best thing you can do for this family is to leave and not come back. Don't tell anyone where you are, don't write and don't call. Just disappear. We've been fine without you so far, and we'll still be fine without you. Nobody cares about you because nobody wants used shoes. You will always be used shoes. The sooner you learn that, the better. So just leave."

I left.

Never had there been a more painful or wasted trip.

Thirteen

Ft. Lauderdale

After the wedding, I returned to Portland an even bigger mess. I felt so unloved, so unwanted, and the only way I could think to handle it was by immersing myself in work. But even that didn't numb the pain.

That next year I left and went to Ft. Lauderdale, Florida for a few months. It was 1980. I got a job at a gay resort there, and since I wasn't twenty-one yet, I worked as a pool towel boy.

Many of the guests that stayed there were from

Hollywood and worked in the adult video industry. I was immediately noticed and became involved, working on videos seven days a week. I made good money, but the job took a lot out of me and I became exhausted physically, mentally, and emotionally. There were also adults parties held on a regular basis, and to get through it all and do what I was being paid to do, I numbed myself by drinking a lot and smoking plenty of marijuana. This was in addition to the prescribed Valium and Xanax I took on a regular basis just to cope day to day. As long as I was sufficiently drugged, I could be whatever they wanted me to be onscreen.

It wasn't long before the hotel was raided and shut down. I didn't get busted, but I was out of a job. This was on Mother's Day and I got a sudden urge to call Mama and wish her a good day. I thought it might cheer me up as well. Despite her hatred, I missed having a family and thought of them all the time. So I picked up the phone and called her.

"Hello."

"Hey, Mama, it's your son, Jimmy."

"I'm sorry, but I don't have a son."

What? "Mama, it's me, Jimmylee, James Bond."

"I'm sorry, but you have the wrong number. Please don't call back again." She hung up.

What the hell . . . I called back. She answered and I said, "Mama, it's me, Jimmy. I'm calling to wish you a Happy Mother's Day and let you know I'm in Ft. Lauderdale, Florida."

"I don't have a son." She again hung up. Her shunning affected me worse than it should have. You would think I would be immune to her hatred, but she was the only mother I had ever known.

Afterward, I walked along the beach and thought of the *Footprints* poem Grandma Grubbs once recited to me.

One night I had a dream--
I dreamed I was walking along the beach with the Lord,
and across the sky flashed scenes from my life.
For each scene I noticed two sets of footprints,
one belonged to me and the other to the Lord.

When the last scene of my life flashed before me,
I looked back at the footprints in the sand.
I noticed that many times along the path of my life,
there was only one set of footprints.

I also noticed that it happened at the very lowest
and saddest times in my life.

This really bothered me and I questioned the Lord about it.
"Lord, you said that once I decided to follow you,
you would walk with me all the way,
but I have noticed that during the most troublesome times in my life
there is only one set of footprints.
I don't understand why in times when I needed you most,
you should leave me."

The Lord replied, "My precious, precious child,
I love you and I would never, never leave you.
during your times of trial and suffering,
when you saw only one set of footprints,
it was then that I carried you."

Pondering the words, I wondered if I was ever carried. Sitting down on the sand, my mind was quickly immersed in thought. I had no idea what I was going to do. I was so lonely, thoughts of suicide crept into my mind. I figured no one would care if I was gone, so what did it matter?

I had too many issues to count. Besides suicidal thoughts, I was constantly worrying about my weight and appearance, so I suffered from eating disorders. In the adult industry, just like modeling, looks and image are everything, and you are always competing because there are always younger, better looking models, and you have to keep up or get left behind.

Glimpsing a broken bottle in the sand, I picked it up and did something I had seen others do, but had never done before myself. I made a small cut on my arm. As I watched the red drip down, the ball of pain inside me slowly eased, and I felt a little more in control. Getting up, I went home, bandaged my arm, and smoked some of my roommate's marijuana.

With nothing holding us in Ft. Lauderdale, we packed our bags and went to Key West where more filming was going on. After a few weeks of this, I was referred to an adult agency on Melrose Place in California by a contact working on the videos.

Heading out, I worked there for a while, then returned to Portland, burned out, but still easily employed.

Fourteen

Jordan Jantz

Back in the heart of things, I hooked up with a few bar owners in Portland. I then started working in underground sex trafficking while working for the escort service. Because of my unique look, I was in demand at the service. I was also still doing runway and catalog for Sears, JC Penny and Montgomery Ward.

I was still hurting a little from Mama's response to my efforts to reach out, and I also missed Daddy. I knew he would be ashamed of my profession, but I still missed being his son.

* * *

The years passed quickly and blurred together because every single day of my life was the same, nothing ever changing. I did the same things, met the same kinds of people, and the friends I made along the way lived lives that mirrored my own. This monotony was all I knew. By now I was hitting thirty and the pattern was set.

It was during this down time that I got to know my neighbor, Greg Jantz. He was a fireman and a staunch Baptist. *And* he liked to party. He said he was a wealth adviser, as well as a spiritual adviser at his Pentecostal church. Greg was very nice to me. There was never anything but friendship between us, but I did set him up with others. His special fetish for a certain type of man was something he kept hidden from his family and church.

I got to know Greg a bit, and after sharing a bit of my life with him, he immediately took me under his wing and became a father figure–which was easy since that was the very thing I was starved for–and I became part of their family. His children were very accepting of me and I grew to care about them a great deal. I chose to ignore the things I knew about Greg that would surely label him a hypocrite. I wanted a family again, and the more time I spent with them, the more attached I became.

To keep his reputation spotless, he got married again and I became attached to his wife as well. I was involved with this family for years. They took me on family vacations. I spent holidays with them, and went to church with them. They were an affluent family, very showy in their dress and the way they carried themselves. And because I was so image-conscious, I fit in well.

I was very happy.

* * *

Then came the day when Greg told me he and his wife wanted to adopt me and change my name to Jordan Jantz; he chose the name Jordan because it meant 'crossing over.' I wasn't so sure about it, and I really didn't want to risk being hurt again. When I told them this, they promised that if I would allow them to change my name, they would never abandon me. They would always be there and I could forever depend on them.

Greg's pleas went on for years. Something inside me kept fighting, making me resist. It was so hard for me to trust. I had been hurt too many times, abandoned by too many people, and mistrust was ingrained in me. So was self-preservation.

Worn down by Greg's repeated tearful promise to never abandon me, I finally relented, *holding* him to that promise.

The family had an adoption celebration for me on Christmas Eve night, and though a small part of me still felt cautious, I was happy to be loved and accepted. They knew what my daily life was like and what I did for a living, yet they still wanted me. Greg asked me to call him dad so I did. Since I lost my own father, he sort of filled in, though I knew I could never be as close to him. Still, this was enough.

* * *

We vacationed in Hawaii one year and the family was given the opportunity be on a Trinity Broadcast evangelical program. Before it was time to go on, Dad said he wanted to talk to me about something. He told me he understood how terrible I had it as a child, and how it led to my present lifestyle, but it was time for things to change, and in order for my soul to be saved, I needed to quit my escorting job and stop being gay. He said he wanted me to stand up in front of the television audience and say I was no longer attracted to men, and then again in front of the church congregation at home. I was supposed to explain that because I was unwanted as a child and my family turned away from me, I turned to men and a life of prostitution. He urged me to tell the congregation that I now had a family that wanted me, that the Jantzs saved me from living a life of tragedy and sin. And because of their unconditional love, I was delivered from evil. I needed to *testify of my new life.*

His request blew me away because it was so unexpected.

I told him I couldn't quit my job or stop what I was doing, because I didn't know how to do anything else. And I definitely was not going to stand in front of the whole church and lie about my feelings. I couldn't possibly turn it off just like that. There was not a switch that I could simply flip and be someone totally different.

He said to me, "You can do this, Jordan. You have to. You need to be saved."

"I can't lie like that," I said. "And I won't stop working for the service."

With a hard look in his eyes, he said, "You do it or else you are no longer a member of the family."

And there it was.

That was the moment of truth.

It was never about loving me. It was about his reputation. It was about making himself and his family look good in the eyes of his church and their circle of friends and acquaintances, despite his own secret doings of the opposite. Greg Jantz never cared about me; he only cared about what adopting me would do for him.

With that truth came the renewal of my loneliness. The ache in my heart was excruciating. It turns out my temporary father had been lying to church members the entire time. I had been used by Greg, just like I was used by everyone else. My trust in his promise to never abandon me was thrown away and I knew things between us would never be the same. And the thought of losing my new siblings amplified the pain. In all my years with them, the Jantz children were never told about my life or what I did for a living.

But during my final vacation with the family, I did tell them. Then I left, carrying a shattered heart.

Fifteen

Breaking Point

With so many things weighing upon me–abandonment, exhaustion from working to pay bills, and having no one I could truly trust–I decided I was done; I was done being hurt. This life held nothing for me.

Walking into my apartment in the wee hours of the morning, I grabbed a rope and a couple of weights. Putting the things in a bag, I left and headed to the Burnside Bridge.

Tying the weights to the ends of the rope and

wrapping it around my neck, I said, "God, I want to leave. I'm tired of the pain and I'm ready to be with you."

Then I jumped off the bridge into the freezing water.

* * *

I awakened three days later in the hospital psychiatric unit completely confused. There were flowers all around the white room, which confused me even more and I wondered if I was in heaven. I didn't know where I was or even *who* I was–meaning I didn't know if I was James, Jimmylee or Jordan. The doctor explained that when the paramedics revived me, I was brought to the hospital and was now in lockdown to keep me from attempting suicide again. He told me I was Jordan Jantz.

I spent two weeks there, undergoing therapy. After sharing my childhood and teen years, I was diagnosed as suffering from multiple personality disorder. The doctor explained that I would disassociate with each traumatic experience and was continually splitting to fit every situation. He wanted to put me under hypnosis and administer a serum to dig deeper into my subconscious, but I said no. There were too many things locked inside me that I didn't want to bring to the surface–many things that I knew happened, but couldn't really remember. Since I was already a wreck that was the last thing I wanted.

While I was there, the Jantz family was called and told what happened. When they finally came to see me–everyone but Greg, that is–I was told to keep this information to myself or they wouldn't have anything to do with me. I didn't see that as a major sacrifice since they'd already abandoned me. When they left that day, it was the last I ever saw of them. I would try to contact them several times in the future, but every letter would be returned. We lived in the same city–and still do.

But to this day, I have no contact with them.

Sixteen

Reunion

Hearing about my twentieth high school reunion, I made a call to see if Tina was registered to attend. She was, so I signed up as well. I also got her contact information and gave her a call. She was completely shocked to hear from me because they all thought I was dead. She broke down and sobbed, then explained about Daddy hiring a private detective to look for me. I didn't tell her that the name change was probably the reason he couldn't find me. I was too ashamed to ever tell anyone.

I told her I would be attending the reunion and asked her not to say anything to Mama or Daddy. She promised she wouldn't and told me about my two little nephews. I couldn't wait to see them.

Before getting off the phone she said, "Jimmy, why did you leave?"

"Because Mama said I was an embarrassment to the family, that you were ashamed of me all through school. Then she told me the best thing I could do for the family would be to leave and not come back."

"It wasn't true," she tearfully told me.

We agreed to meet when I got there. I traveled with some friends and we stayed in a motel just outside of the city. I was so nervous about seeing Tina–excited but nervous.

Tina and I held each other and cried. We caught up on everything and I finally shared with her what I dealt with as a kid. She asked me why I never told her. I said I didn't want her to know because I was ashamed and afraid, not only that Uncle Arthur would hurt her, but that she would no longer love me. She assured me that would never happen. I accepted that, but I had heard those words too many times to ever completely trust them again.

I had a great time at the reunion. It was good to see my old school mates, and I was really happy to see one in particular. Shawn was an old friend and my next door neighbor. She knew and witnessed much of the abuse I suffered from Mama. As we talked, she told me how awful it was hearing my screams coming from the garage, and she was sorry for what I went through. I really appreciated knowing she cared.

* * *

It was hard saying goodbye to Tina because I didn't know when, or if, I would see her again. I made no promises and neither did she, but knowing that we were both still existing in the world was enough for us.

I pondered my life on the way back to Portland. It was filled with pornography, prostitution, phone sex, meeting in adult bookstores. I'd had sex in every place imaginable–public restrooms, in malls and alleys. It was an automatic function with no off switch.

And when there was no one to be with, there was self-gratification while viewing images in pornographic magazines. That was the lifestyle. It wasn't a life of simply getting together for fun. It was one of cocktails and immorality, all for a few minutes to an hour of pleasure.

Then it was on to the next person, hoping this one would be *the one* you wanted to spend the rest of your life with. I was lonely and emotionally messed up. I *knew* this. I had friends, yes, but no solid relationships to ground me. I think a part of me was searching for something, anything that would give me a sense of belonging.

Seventeen

Mark

During the mid 90s, I was working a weekend runway show for a new season of designer swimwear, and was grateful to still have normal above-board paying gigs. That night after the show, I went to a gay club with some friends and met Mark. He was a model, very good looking, and he turned the heads of both men and women. Getting to know him, I discovered he was one of the kindest and most decent people I had ever met. He was a part-time student and ten years younger than me, but the age difference didn't matter to either of us. He gave me a ride home that night and asked if he could see me again. I said yes.

We soon grew closer and began to spend a lot of time together. Mark became very important to me, yet I held back many things about myself. I could tell he held back a little as well, but I was in no position to complain. He was smart and educated and I was inadequate, but garnering his attention made me feel important and special. Being in a business where I was forced to fake intelligence when it came to many things–I was still not functioning well when it came to knowledge of things others take for granted–it was nice to be able to be myself with him.

Mark and I talked about so many things, but I wasn't a person who shared much about my life. I kept many secrets from friends because in the past, so many of them abandoned me for my choices. I didn't want to risk losing Mark's friendship. He was the best person I had ever known, treating me with a gentleness and care I had never received from anyone.

The weeks of friendship grew into something more and we became involved. Though I had been with a few others regularly in the past, what I had with

Mark was entirely different and I actually felt loved. Not just used, but really loved. It was an indescribable feeling.

But Mark knew there was something different about me. He knew I was holding back. He also knew not to push. He simply let me know that he cared and would be there for me.

* * *

One day Mark shared something that completely shocked me.

"Jordan, I need to tell you something."

"Okay."

"I'm LDS."

"What is that?"

"I'm Mormon."

Oh, my hell! "You're a man of the cloth?"

He smiles. "I'm a returned missionary."

Thinking about it a moment, I said, "Well, it's okay, but I have to tell you, I'm not into that, so just don't go weird on me, okay?"

"Okay."

Knowing Mark's background only brought us closer, and I now understood why he was so polite and good. He was my best friend, and I never wanted to do anything to ruin that. I promised him that what he'd shared with me would stay just between us. I would never tell anyone. And because he'd trusted me enough to open himself so fully, I shared the details of my life, including currently making a living not only modeling, but as a paid escort. He told me he loved me and didn't care.

* * *

After a couple of years together, Mark introduced me to his Mormon family. Since the day he'd told them he was gay, Mark and his family had grown apart and he only saw them once or twice a year. I always hated religious people, because the ones I knew were so judgmental, but I did respect Mark's family because they were *his* family. Still, at times, it hurt to see him sink into bouts of depression about not being close to them. He wasn't the son they thought he should be and would never fit their idea of a perfect man.

I finally said to him one day, "They are going to make you crazy if you don't stop loving them so much. They only love you for show. They are 'Plastic

Fantastic' religious people." He hated hearing this because it was the truth. I told him I would never let religion in my life because I had seen what these so-called Christians did to people. In their eyes, we would never measure up. I don't know if he agreed, but he understood. He understood *me,* and why I felt that way. And that was what mattered.

Mark and I were together for years, never actually living together but seeing each other every day. Sometimes it was very hard to be with him, because he would read the Book of Mormon and then be intimate with me afterward. I was completely confused by this. You see, Mark loved God so much. But he was gay and a Mormon. How could this be? How could he choose to live both standards?

I sheltered him from my friends because I knew he would never fit into that world and they would never accept him. He was everything that was good. Still, I could never give myself completely because of the way my life was. I had a plan and I wasn't going to change it for anyone. As messed up as I was, I still had a set way my life would go.

* * *

The relationship slowly started going south.

Mark asked me one day, "Jordan, would you be willing to let go of the life you have planned for yourself and embrace the one that is waiting for you?"

Thinking he was trying to change me, I was offended. "Never, Mark," I answered. "Not for you or anyone else."

We had spent the last seven years together. Mark's family thought he was evil and thought I was even worse. And I wanted out. So one day I told him, "It's my way or the highway." I asked him to leave my life.

And he did.

I didn't see Mark again for almost two years, but I never stopped thinking about him. Before him, no one had ever stayed with me. I was used to people walking in and out of my life. This fact only served to point out how much my actions had been spurred on by fear–fear that he would one day leave like the rest.

So I left him first.

Eighteen

The Test Came Back Positive

I made many more connections through the years working in the adult industry–political figures, Hollywood directors, mafia members–and those connections stayed with me, turning into friends who became important to me.

One of these particular connections was made when I met a client at a hotel who turned out to be an undercover cop. When I came out of the bathroom prepared to entertain, I was arrested and taken to jail. Needless to say, I was in shock because this had never happened to me before. Many of my clients were on the police force and some worked for the academy. I also had many clients in the medical and law profession. All of these people took care of me. Because of this, I was released from jail and my record was expunged, so I was able to continue working. However, it was during that time that I tested positive for AIDS.

AIDS.

Those four letters changed everything.

I could no longer work for the escort service, and since I had never held a regular job before, or even learned how to fill out an application, the only income I had coming in was from sparse modeling jobs with companies that I was still under contract with. I also did some table pole dancing in a shady restaurant just to pay the bills. The sleeping around portion of my life was history, so now I was strictly entertaining, nothing more. It's amazing how one diagnosis can alter the course of a life so completely.

* * *

I contacted my family to tell them I was sick. Mama still wanted nothing to do with me and even told Daddy I had died.

I did eventually see Daddy again. He and his wife were living in Nevada and the reunion was bittersweet. I admitted that I had AIDS and felt ashamed. I didn't tell him how I caught it because I didn't feel the need to share that, or any other things about my life. Daddy told me more about how he'd hired a private investigator to look for me. I still didn't have the heart or the courage to tell him my name was changed. We reminisced over our life together, sharing memories and experiences of the past. He told me many times that he was sorry about how hard my childhood was and I assured him he had nothing to be sorry for. He was the best father I could ever ask for.

I had a wonderful visit with my dad. And though I would still have contact with him for years to come, that particular visit will stay with me forever.

* * *

I started getting sick pretty quickly, and for the the next few years I was in an AIDS hospice, going through blood transfusions and treatments. It was horrifying to discover that my life was no longer mine. I felt like I had lost everything. My priorities started changing in a major way.

I constantly thought of my family and wished things had been different between us. I also began to think of God a little more. I had always believed in God, I just didn't think he was there for me much. But then again, how could he be, with the way I had lived my life? I knew what happened in my childhood wasn't my fault, but as I grew older, my choices were my own. Still, I think deep down, there was a small part of me that believed God watched over me, and probably cried over my choices, too.

* * *

Lying in my room thinking about life and how much time I had left, I was surprised to see two young men in white shirts and ties standing in my doorway. They asked if they could come in and visit. They looked like insurance salesmen.

Swearing inwardly, I let them in, but I told them up front I wasn't into whatever they were selling. I then asked them who they were.

One responded, "We are missionaries from The Church of Jesus Christ of Latter-Day Saints."

Inside I was freaking out. I couldn't believe it.

Missionaries from the Mormon church are sitting in my room?

They asked if they could come by and see me that week. I can't say why I did, but I said yes.

* * *

I only saw these missionaries a couple of times. They were a little too pushy–maybe because I was so far gone health-wise. I wasn't interested in talking to them again, and I told them I didn't want anymore discussions.

Nineteen

Persistence Softens a Heart

Christmas was coming and my health had improved. I was doing a lot better and getting ready to move into an apartment when the second set of missionaries started coming by. One of them, Elder Wallentine, said they just stopped by to say hello and bring me a gift. I said okay, but I was still confused over the whole Mormon thing. I thought about Mark and his struggles, and I didn't want to be like that–depressed because of trying to live two lifestyles.

I said to the Elder, "I'll give you a year to be a

part of my life. In return, I'll be part of yours. I'll take your lessons and listen to what you have to say. Just don't tell me I'm going to hell because I'm gay."

And they agreed. The following day, Elder Wallentine called and told me how much it meant to them that I had been so open and real. I continued seeing the missionaries and their messages began to touch something deep inside me.

However, all was not smooth sailing. It was hard to leave a life that had been such a major part of me for so long. Sometimes the missionaries would show up and find me drunk or strung out on coke. I was still supporting myself by stripping and pole dancing. Getting high was the only way I was able to get in front of men and do this.

They never judged me and never gave up. Elder Wallentine assured me repeatedly that they loved me and would be there no matter what.

I'd heard that phrase so many times and was always lied to.

But I believed *him*.

I *really* believed him.

It wasn't their words, but their actions that

convinced me. I was a gay man with AIDS, stripping in bars each night and living a terrible life, but they never faltered in their friendship.

They were truly living their religion.

Over the next while, I came to experience moments of peace. The feeling was completely foreign because there had never been any peace in my life. Despite my conflicted emotions, I couldn't deny that what I had been taught about the Savior and His love for me was true. I came to believe God knew me and what I had gone through. He had only been waiting for me to open to Him. God had witnessed my childhood and felt anger in my behalf. He'd also witnessed my choices and His Son paid for them with His blood.

I felt so ashamed and wished I could go back and change the things I'd done. But that wasn't possible. All I could do was let it all go and move on.

* * *

Mark and I had been seeing each other again for a while, but our relationship was only one of friendship. When I finally called him one day and shared my experiences with the missionaries, he cried and said he did not want to see me hurt by the Church the way he was. I told him that though I would always love him, I had to do this. I had to make this change. I *needed* to do it.

"If you can't accept this," I finally said, "then there will never be anything between us again." And because he didn't want to lose my friendship, he accepted my choice. Again, he was kind to me.

As for me, after having a taste of the gospel, I could truly understand why Mark was such a good person. He was raised to be a Christian, became gay, and suddenly his supposed 'Christian' family wanted nothing to do with him.

Sadly, Mark was the only true Christian in that family.

Twenty

I'll Never Forget

After a year of taking the discussions from the missionaries, I prayed to God and said, "If you love me and really won't leave me like other people who called themselves Christians, I will be baptized into your church. If you love me, please show me this is all real."

He answered my prayer. Getting a sweet, peaceful confirmation, I made the decision and was baptized.

Mark was very upset. Still, he came to my baptism to support me, along with many of my gay and straight friends and acquaintances. They were all surprised, but wanted to be there for me. I appreciated that more than I could possibly say.

Not long after that day, things with Mark became more strained. When I stopped by to see him again, he said he was afraid the Church would take me away from him. I tried to stress the importance of our friendship and how much he meant to me. He didn't want to hear anything I had to say, and because he wouldn't accept my decision, or my friendship, I ended the relationship. It was a painful decision, but I wanted to be a man of God and go to heaven when I died. I was so sorry for the way things turned out, but I finally understood that life was too short, and I was finished wishing for love. God needed me to be better and I wanted to be better. I said goodbye to Mark and left.

I knew that as hard as it would be, I could never look back. That closet door was closed forever.

* * *

It was Christmas Day, and though I was spending it alone, I had a gift for Mark and decided to take it to him. I figured that if he was still angry and threw it back in my face, at least he'd know I hadn't forgotten about him. My heart considered it my one last attempt to say I was sorry and move on.

When I knocked on the door and he didn't answer–I had given my key back long ago–I asked the landlord to let me in so I could leave the gift. I sat on the couch in the living room, deciding to wait for him. I wanted to watch him open it and let him know he would always have a place in my heart.

After a short while, I went to use his bathroom, looking around as I went. He was a neat person and always kept a clean place.

When I open the bathroom door, the world stopped and everything inside me immediately died. Mark's body was hanging in the shower, his eyes open and glazed over.

He killed himself.

I started crying and screaming, yelling at the top of my lungs, "Please, God, no! Please no!"

Running downstairs to the landlord's apartment, I banged on the door and the police were quickly called. My emotions were out of control and I couldn't think. The sight of Mark's body hanging in the shower was branded in my head, and I knew it would never go away.

When the paramedics arrived and declared him dead, I was so freaked out I couldn't even speak. Over and over I asked God why this happened. All I could think about was how hurt Mark had been, by me, his family, everyone, but his family most of all.

That night, I called Mark's parents and told them about his suicide. Their response was, "Well, Mark was a depressed gay man," like it was bound to happen. I couldn't believe it! He had been a missionary, was a good and decent person with so much love to give, and they considered him hopeless. They then said that because he left the Church and his family, he should be cremated so he could continue being 'a proud gay man.'

To which I responded, "No, you're so wrong. You left your son, but he never left you. He never stopped loving his family, and you did nothing but preach at him and tell him how terrible he was. Love is supposed to be unconditional. He made choices you didn't agree with, but you abandoned him because of them. Who was more wrong?"

* * *

They did indeed have him cremated. Then they

met me and gave me his ashes.

Taking them to the beach by my home, I tearfully sprinkled them into the river and said an emotional goodbye to my friend, keeping a prayer in my heart that I would one day see him again.

I'll never forget that Christmas or the person I loved so much. He was the best friend I had ever had. We shared a love that was never spoken of because I'd always honored his secrecy. I knew I would never love anyone like that again. Not only because the lifestyle I lived for so many years was no longer mine, but also because Mark's loss helped me to know with absolute certainty that I needed to hold to my new-found faith and let go of the painful, hurtful things I had experienced *and* witnessed people do to each other. People don't understand that though a heart may be broken in different ways, it keeps beating just the same.

I knew Mark was at peace. He was with God and would never feel rejected again. His love for God had such an impact on my life. I just wished I could have told him. I wished he could have handled the trials placed upon him, that we could have helped each other.

I wished for so many things . . .

A life changed.

Me and my service dog, Charity.

With Spencer Wallentine and his father, Kent

Wallentine Family Vacation

2012

My Family

I
Thank
You
2012

Epilogue

And Here I Am

How do you piece together a life that was never whole to begin with?

How do you get past experiences and events of such magnitude and start again?

Simply put, you put all in order and let go.

I did eventually see Mama and my biological family again. Surprisingly, Mama moved out east and they now lived in the same state. Going back to Illinois, I got to know my father and his sister. That was the only good thing that came of it.

Other than that, neither experience was pleasant. Both brought a new layer of the same old lies, deceits, and hatefulness. My kindness and efforts to reach out were spat back in my face, because none were willing to accept their part in shaping my childhood. So I chose to bid those experiences a proper farewell by never thinking on them again. None of it matters now.

What does matter is nothing can ever be hidden from God, no matter how hard we try to hide it, or how deep we attempt to bury it.

People don't think children can remember things that happen at such a young age, but they do. We all remember things from those young years. And while there are many things that are blocked and hidden in my subconscious, I remember the things that matter.

I remember being told that I was ugly, and in order for people to love me, I needed to be the best little boy in the world.

In order to make it in life and be somebody, I needed to be the best little boy in the world.

In order to be loved enough for someone to stay, I needed to be the best little boy in the world.

I was never taught that, to God, I have always

been the best little boy in the world, along with every other little child. I was the best by simply being me, James Lee Bond, then Jimmylee.

That trained mindset stayed with me through my twenties, thirties and forties. I am almost fifty-four now, and I am finally starting to shed the idea that was ingrained in me all those years ago.

So, now I try to focus on where I am at this moment, not where I was. I don't know what will happen tomorrow or in the future. I only know that as long as I stay on the path that has been placed before me, I will be okay. As long as I hold on to my Savior's hand, He will hold on to mine and never let go. I can honestly say that for the first time in my life, His is truly one hand that has not let go. If He had, I wouldn't be here now.

Because I had so much support from the gay community, I found it hard to leave that support behind. Once you are a part of the life, it is difficult to let go. Many of my dear friends have remained in the community. Unfortunately, many of them have also passed away. They thought they would live forever, but they had been mistaken.

As far gone as I once was, it is truly a miracle that I am still here. Homosexual friends tell me even now, "Jordan, if you can do this, anyone can." I hope and pray that I can in some way help them accomplish the same.

These days I spend my time doing what I can to share God's message with others by sharing my life and the miracles He has wrought in me. I do this by speaking to church congregations and large groups all over Portland. When I can, I take the message outside of Oregon. Like Moses in the Bible, I am not mighty in speaking, and this is definitely the last thing I ever expected to be doing. I never expected to live long enough to accomplish any of the things I have since giving my life to God.

But *He* had a plan of His own for me. And I will be here until my work on this earth is finished.

I have made many new friends in this new life. And there is one friend I will be forever grateful for, because he didn't give up on me. Elder Spencer Wallentine and his family have taken me into their hearts and are some of the dearest people in the world to me. They know the kind of life I once lived, yet there is no judgment. They simply love like a true Christian family should, and my visits with them in Utah, just doing simple everyday things that most people take for granted, are better than any exotic place I've ever been. I will always be thankful to have them in my life.

I am a person who goes all the way or not at all, and I have embraced this new life God has given me with my whole heart. I am still challenged with the residue of my childhood and past–multiple personality and anxiety disorder–and I don't know if those effects will ever go away, but I do know this: when I'm feeling afraid and anguished over darkness seeping from under that locked closet door, all I need to do is remind myself that God has seen it all, and my Savior has born every pain trapped behind it. So I simply throw it open, knowing nothing is hidden, and the small square of darkness is now lit by Christlike love.

And I never need to be afraid again.

Another Word

Jordan gave an amazing prayer during a speaking engagement at an LDS Church in Provo, Utah. It was such a special blessing, I felt inspired to share it. His story wouldn't be complete without it because of how far he has come. He possesses a strong spirit and his testimony of our Heavenly Father's love grows in intensity with each passing day.

These are Jordan's words:

Heavenly Father,

We come to You tonight and ask that You send down your Holy Spirit upon us. Father, You know our

hearts. You know what we think, You know what we do, You know the number of hairs on our heads. You knew us before we even came to this planet. You knew the destiny of our life and what it would be like. You knew the trials that we would go through. So many of us continue to hold onto things every day. Whether we are gay or straight, we all have our addictions and we hold onto them.

Father, there are things in our life that we want to let go. We've been holding onto them for so long that they have torn our spirit, causing deep depression, causing suicidal thoughts, causing us to do things, Father, that we would never do. But we do them in secret. You know we do. You know how hard the struggle has been for each of us here tonight, or we would not be here. We are here, Father, because You give us hope. You give us a future. Some of us feel there is no future and we will have this thorn in our side until the day we die.

So we ask You, Father, right now, through the power of the Holy Ghost, that You would send each person here an angel to walk beside them, for You know we can talk to those angels, because even though they are not visible, they are there. We ask You, Father, to take the weaknesses we harbor away. No matter what our weakness or addiction is, Father, Your Son atoned for us, and You do not condemn us, but You beg us to call upon You.

Father, we are now saying vocally that we no longer want to hold on to the things that are holding us back from being the men and women You have called us to be. We ask you, Father, to take the very things that hold us back, that keep us from growing and being the people You called us to be. We thank You, Father, for sending Your Son, Jesus Christ, to die on the cross for us. We want to nail that cross to the very things that hold us back from achieving our final destination.

Father, will You please take control of our life and take away the things that keep us from being obedient to You? We love You and know You are our God, and Your Son is our Savior. We thank You and ask You in Jesus' name to remove this heavy burden that holds us down, and we give it to You. We surrender it through the power of the Holy Spirit. In Jesus' name we pray. Amen.

Walking Among Angels
Angel
Series
2012

Jordan's Acknowledgments

My eternal gratitude goes to my friend and author, Jewel Adams, for encouraging, supporting and cheering me on in this journey. I thank her for opening the closet doors of my life, and having the patience to work through the multiple personalities, as well as the lingering effects of sexual abuse and abandonment that paralyzes me to this very day–a condition that there is no cure for, except years of medication and therapy. Jewel's desire to do my biography started out as a gift to others, but became a gift to me. Doing something kind for another person can transform you in unimaginable ways. I will always be grateful to my beautiful friend for traveling back into the many closet doors of my life.

I am grateful for my medical support team that has been my advocate since I am not able to defend myself. I no longer feel like a pair of used shoes. I continue to receive the highest quality of medical service today, for which I am grateful. If I didn't have doctors working with me on a weekly basis, my life would be unmanageable, and I would be dead. I am so grateful to God for placing them in my life. They have continued to work with me for fourteen of the thirty-four years I have lived in Portland.

To running Bull, I will never forget you. I will always be your Swift Arrow. The Colorado River is our river. It will always be special to me. It is a place of peace and beauty, just the way my life was with you in it. You gave me the most positive impression of a father's heart I could ever hope to have, and I have always loved you. We will be together again in heaven, and we will be a forever family that no one can separate.

I spent my life in fear. Therefore, courage and dignity were my only attributes for survival. These trials transformed me, and many of my problems were endurable because of the many Gay and Lesbian brothers and sisters who have walked through therapy with me when family abandoned me for reasons that will never be known. I love these brothers and sisters, and I know God loves them, too. He is not a respecter of persons. Thank-you, my straight and gay family, for not abandoning me. Your memories are with me forever.

To my brothers and sisters in the LDS church, God has knitted us out of the same cloth. Thank you for your prayers of healing and restoration for my life. You have a major place in my heart. I never felt like I was a piece of the puzzle before, but now I know the puzzle won't ever be completed unless we're all together. Every member in our spiritual family is valuable to me.

Finally, there are too many people to thank for the evolution of this book than I can possibly name. I offer a collective prayer of thanks to them all, and I hope they realize that though names are not mentioned, it does not diminish my gratitude for the integrated power of prayer and the practice of medicine that make my life as full and abundant as possible. The physicians that practice prayer give me hope that my life can be an example to others.

A Final Thought

If you are struggling with a painful past that has led you down a destructive path, there is a way out. You have been blessed with the gift of choice, and that gift can lead you to great things, as well as a new life–one that will be more glorious than you can possibly imagine. But it is up to you to make it happen.

We hope this book will motivate you in that quest. No matter what your situation is, there are so many others who are struggling with the same trials. There will always be challenges, and since you can't change the past, just concentrate on today. Because the choices you make today will be the ones that will affect your future. Yes, the pain from yesterday's trials and mistakes will always be remembered, but it is how you allow those trials to affect you and what you do with them that counts.

About the Writing of This Book

This was the most challenging project I have ever taken on. Much of Jordan's story came from recordings we made in my library. After four days of listening to the indescribable experiences of his life, I had the challenging task of piecing everything together, which was no small feat. The whole experience was emotionally draining and some days I wondered if I would be able to finish it. But with God's help I did, and this book is the most rewarding thing I have ever done. I feel blessed and grateful for the opportunity to participate in a work that will touch hearts and change lives.

In writing this book the privacy and regulations of The Americans with Disabilities Act has been followed.

Author of Jordan's book
Jewel Adams book signing 2014

Jordan's Voices
of Hope 2014
Producer and brother, Ty

About the Author

J. Adams is the author of interracial and young adult inspirational romance, as well as a motivational speaker. She and her husband are the parents of eight children and grandparents of seven and counting. In her spare time (when she has any) she likes to curl up with a good book and a healthy stash of orange Tic Tacs. She resides in Utah. If you would like to drop her a line, you can reach her at jewela40@gmail.com

Website: JewelAdams.com

Blogs:

jordans-light.blogspot.com

jewelsbestgems.blogspot.com